STAMP COLL

HOW TO IDENT⌐⌐ ⌐⌐AMPS

COMPILED BY
JAMES WATSON

STANLEY GIBBONS PUBLICATIONS LTD LONDON AND RINGWOOD

Published by **Stanley Gibbons Publications Ltd**
Editorial, Sales Offices and Distribution Centre:
5 Parkside, Christchurch Road, Ringwood,
Hants BH24 3SH

© *Stanley Gibbons Publications Ltd 1988*

First Published 1983
Reprinted, with amendments 1986
Second edition 1988
Reprinted with amendments 1991

Also in this series

Stamp Collecting—**How To Start**
Stamp Collecting—**Collecting By Theme**
Stamp Collecting—**How to Arrange and Write Up a Stamp Collection**
Stamp Collecting—**Philatelic Terms Illustrated**
Stamp Collecting—**The Stanley Gibbons Guide to Stamp Collecting**

The Compiler: the late James Watson joined the staff of Stanley Gibbons in 1946 and worked in the New Issues Dept. before becoming a feature writer for Gibbons Stamp Monthly. *He retired from Gibbons in 1981. Mr. Watson wrote several books on philately—most notably the* Stanley Gibbons Book of Stamps and Stamp Collecting. *He also wrote about cine photography and was an expert on picture postcards of the early 20th century.*

Second edition, revised by John Holman, Editor of Gibbons Stamp Monthly, *1985–88.*

Designed by Julia Lilauwala.

Printed in Great Britain by BAS Printers Limited, Over Wallop, Hampshire.

ISBN 0-85259-042-3

S.G. Item No. 2761

CONTENTS

INTRODUCTION

You may wonder why this little guide is necessary to help you to identify your stamps. Surely, you think, most postage stamps bear the names of the countries issuing them. It is true that many stamps can be recognised by the name of the country imprinted upon them, but the point is that the stamps of many foreign countries are *not* inscribed with the English names we know so well. Some are not even in the familiar Roman alphabet, and sometimes the inscriptions on a stamp bewilder the experts!

Japan

    Ideally, this guide should be used with the *Stanley Gibbons Simplified Catalogue of Stamps of the World*, which is now published in two volumes. Identification is the key to the catalogue as you must be able to recognise the country which has issued a stamp before you can look it up in the catalogue. Conversely, the catalogue is also the key to identification because it records some 270,000 stamps with a substantial number of illustrations, and a nodding acquaintance with the pattern and style of different countries' stamps will be of great assistance to identification of your own stamps. The main elements of a stamp design which provide clues to identity are the country name, subordinate or secondary inscriptions, national emblems or symbols and the currency or face value.

    'Helvetia', for example, is the Latin name for Switzerland and it is used regularly on Swiss stamps. The chrysanthemum emblem appeared on Japanese stamps from 1872 to about 1947, while the modern issues are additionally inscribed 'Nippon', which is the Japanese name for Japan. Sometimes the actual design of a stamp indicates a particular country or at least the region of its location. The heraldic eagle relates to central Europe and as a design subject it will lead (supported by the inscriptions) to the identification of the early stamps of Austria ('KKPOST' or 'KREUZER'), Germany

Austria

Germany

Poland

('Deutsches Reich' or 'Reichspost'), Poland ('Poczta Polska') and possibly Albania, Finland and Russia. Centimes and francs indicate a French-speaking country; öre and krone (or krona) are Scandinavian; centavos and pesetas or pesos appear on Spanish and Latin-American stamps.

Scandinavian

Latin-American

KEY INSCRIPTIONS

Hindi

By 'inscriptions' we mean all the words and figures appearing on the stamp in addition to the design. For purposes of identification the most important words are those representing the country of issue, which may appear in the normal alphabet (like our own A, B, C . . .), though maybe in a foreign language; in the Cyrillic or Greek alphabets; or in other alphabets and scripts such as Arabic (which looks rather like 'shorthand'), Chinese, Korean and Japanese, Hindi (the devanagari script of India), and Urdu and Bengali (Pakistan). Urdu has many Arabic and Persian words, while Persian, with Pushtu, is also the written language of Afghanistan. Malay is the language of the natives of the Malay Archipelago and islands of South-east Asia (Malaysia) and has Arabic elements infused. The Siamese language (of the inhabitants of Thailand) is derived from a form of Sanscrit, and has affinities with Chinese. Hebrew is the official language of modern Israel, and Amharic is the official tongue of Ethiopia.

Korean

Bengali

Amharic

Chinese

Japanese

Malay

Siamese

Hebrew

British stamps show only the monarch's head. A silhouette is usually shown on special stamps (left)

Fortunately many of these countries additionally inscribe their stamps in the normal alphabet, while some even use the recognisable English versions, such as 'Israel' and 'Thailand'. Great Britain is the only country in the world which enjoys the privilege, granted by universal accord as the inventor of the postage stamp, of omitting the country name though, since the famous Penny Black of 1840, our stamps have borne a portrait of the reigning sovereign. New collectors will soon become familiar with the heads of Queen Victoria, King Edward VII, King George V, King Edward VIII, King George VI and our present Queen Elizabeth II, which also appear on many of the stamps of the Commonwealth territories. In recent times the head of the Queen has been shown in simplified form on G.B. commemorative issues, often just as a silhouette.

Switzerland

Brazil

Finland

Portugal

In early days, before the Universal Postal Union was founded, other countries sometimes omitted their names. These include Austria, Bosnia and Herzegovina, Brazil, Finland, Hungary, the Papal States, Portugal, Sardinia and Spain. The early postage dues of Switzerland comprised figures of value only. On the other stamps the principal clues are the figures of value and/or the portraits depicted on them. Examples are illustrated above.

USING THE CATALOGUE

As its name implies, the *Stanley Gibbons Simplified Catalogue of Stamps of the World* is extremely simple to use. The countries are arranged in alphabetical order and each country title is followed by a reference indicating the section or part of the main catalogue which contains the full detailed listing, and by summarised notes of the country's location, status and currency. Then the lists of stamps follow in chronological order, that is, according to the dates of issue of the stamps, from the earliest to the most recent. Each issue or set is headed by an illustration which has its own number (known as the 'Type number'), and next comes the list of stamps with its descriptive heading and year of issue. If there is no such description of an event or commemoration, it can generally be assumed that the stamps are definitive or regular issues.

Each stamp has its own number, by which it is known and identified by all collectors and dealers who use the catalogue, and each country has its own series of numbers. Next to the stamp number, shown in the first (left-hand) column is the Type number, but if a particular stamp is not illustrated (usually only the first stamp in a set is shown), then a dash is shown, the different designs being listed below. Blanks in this column indicate that all the stamps in the set have the same design as the illustrated stamp or type. Next again are the face values and colours of the stamps with their prices—unused (first column) and used (second column).

The Tristan da Cunha stamp has a modern appearance and also depicts Queen Elizabeth II in silhouette in the top right-hand corner. Reference to the catalogue tells you that the stamp is the first or lowest value in a set of 'Bird' definitives issued in 1977. There are twelve stamps in the set and the style of listing is as follows:

28. BLACK HAGLET

1977 Birds. Multicoloured.
220 1p. Type **28**
221 2p. White-faced Skipjack
222 3p. Stinker
223 4p. Littlest White-breasted Haglet
224 5p. Gony
225 10p. Blue Nighthawk
226 15p. King bird
227 20p. Petrel
228 25p. Nightbird
229 50p. Sea Hen
230 £1 Flying Pinnamin
231 £2 Molly
The 3p. to £2 designs are vertical.

31. KLIPFISH

As all the above stamps are multicoloured there was no need to repeat the colours against each stamp, those spaces being used for the design details. A little further on in your catalogue you will find a set of 'Fishes' with a slightly different arrangement:

1978 Fish
246 **31** 5p. black, brown and green
247 — 10p. black, brown and green
248 — 15p. multicoloured
249 — 20p. multicoloured
Designs: 10p. 'Fivefinger'; 15p. 'Concha'; 20p. 'Soldier'.

Knowing the country obviously eases the task of locating a particular stamp in the catalogue—look for similarities of design, subject and style. And of course you will then know exactly which stamps you need to complete a set, while the detailed information about the stamps and their designs will assist you in writing-up your collection. Just browsing through the catalogue will help you enormously in getting to know the 'look' of a stamp and its various inscriptions. Most countries maintain a distinctive style of design which is easily recognizable and many of the stamps you want to identify will be illustrated. If the actual stamp is not shown you should be able to track down similar characteristics of design. Once you establish the country the rest should be straightforward. Once established, catalogue numbers are rarely changed—usually only when new stamps are added to an existing range of definitives and the lists have to be renumbered to accommodate them. The changes take effect when a new edition of a catalogue is published.

Non Postage Stamps

Collectors will frequently find 'stamps' that are not listed in the *Stamps of the World* catalogue. These are usually fiscal or revenue stamps, locals, telegraph stamps or souvenir labels of one kind or another. Some information about them can be found in the 'Information for Users' section of the catalogue and further details in Chapter 12 of the Stanley Gibbons book *Stamp Collecting: A Guide to Modern Philately.* Such 'stamps' are normally referred to as 'cinderellas' and can form the basis of a sideline collection.

The Gibbons catalogue only lists stamps issued for postal purposes by official postal administrations.

THE NORMAL ALPHABET
A. Country Names: Europe

Bavaria

Andorre. ANDORRA (French Post Offices).
Bayern. BAVARIA. Now part of West Germany.
België/Belgique. BELGIUM. Flemish/French inscriptions.
Böhmen und Mähren. BOHEMIA AND MORAVIA. German protectorate issues.
Bosnien Hercegovina (or **Herzegowina**). BOSNIA AND HERZEGOVINA. Military Post.
Braunschweig. BRUNSWICK. Now part of West Germany.

Bosnia and Herzegovina

Brunswick

Čechy a Morava. BOHEMIA AND MORAVIA. German protectorate issues.
Ceskoslovensko. CZECHOSLOVAKIA.
Confoederatio Helvetica. SWITZERLAND. 'National Fete' issues, etc. 1938–1952.
Danmark. DENMARK.
Deutsche Bundespost. GERMANY. West German issues.
Deutsche Bundespost Berlin. GERMANY. West Berlin issues.
Deutsche Demokratische Republik. GERMANY. East German issues.
Deutsche Post. GERMANY. Post-war issues.
Deutsche Reichspost/Deutsches Reich. GERMANY. 'Empire' issues, 1872–87 and 1902–43.
Deutschösterreich. AUSTRIA. Issues of 1918–20.
Drzavna Posta Hrvatska. YUGOSLAVIA. Croatian issues, 1918–19.
Drzava SHS. YUGOSLAVIA. Slovenian issues, 1919–20.
Eesti. ESTONIA. Now part of the Soviet Union.
Eire. IRELAND (REPUBLIC).

Greenland

Switzerland

Ireland

Faroe Islands

España. SPAIN.
Føroyar. FAROE ISLANDS. A Danish possession.
Grønland. GREENLAND. A Danish possession.
Grossdeutsches Reich. GERMANY. Nazi issues, 1943–45.
Haute-Silésie. UPPER SILESIA. Plebiscite issues, 1920–22.
Helvetia. SWITZERLAND.

Lithuania

Hungary

Poland

Hrvatska. CROATIA.
Island. ICELAND.
Italia/Poste Italiane. ITALY.
Jugoslavija. YUGOSLAVIA.
Kraljevstvo (or Kraljevina) Srba, Hrvata i Slovenaca. YUGOSLAVIA, 1921–31.
Latvija (or Latwija). LATVIA. Now part of the Soviet Union.
Lietuva. LITHUANIA. Now part of the Soviet Union.
Litwa Srodkowa. CENTRAL LITHUANIA. Independence issues of 1920–22.
Magyar Kir. Posta/Magyar Posta/Magyarorszag. HUNGARY.
Nations Unies. UNITED NATIONS — Geneva Headquarters.
Nederland. NETHERLANDS. Also called HOLLAND.
Norge/Noreg. NORWAY.
Norddeutscher Postbezirk. NORTH GERMAN CONFEDERATION.
Orts-Post. 'Local Post'. SWITZERLAND 1850.
Österreich/Oesterreich. AUSTRIA.
Ottomanes, Postes. TURKEY 1914.
Poczta Polska/Polska. POLAND.
Pohjois Inkeri. NORTH INGERMANLAND. Part of Russia.
Poste Locale. SWITZERLAND 1850.
Preussen. PRUSSIA.
Rayon. SWITZERLAND 1850–54.
Reichspost. GERMANY. Empire issues, 1889–1901.
République Française/Repub. Franc. FRANCE.
Rheinland-Pfalz. GERMANY. Allied Occupation 1947–49.
Romagne, Franco Bollo Postale. ROMAGNA. Former Papal State.
Romana/Romina. RUMANIA.
S. Marino, Repubblica (or Rep.) di. SAN MARINO.
Saargebiet. SAAR. Now part of Germany.
Sachsen. SAXONY.
Saorstat Eireann 1922. IRELAND (REPUBLIC). 'Irish Free State'.
Shqipenia. ALBANIA, 1913–20.
Shqipenie. ALBANIA, 1920–22.
(Posta) Shqyptare. ALBANIA, 1922–25, 1930.
R.E.P. (or Republika) Shqiptare. ALBANIA, 1925–30, 1939–43.
Shqipni. ALBANIA, 1937–38.
Shqipnija. ALBANIA, 1944, 1947.
Republika Popullore e or R.P.S.E. Shqiperise. ALBANIA, 1946–.
Shquiperia. ALBANIA, 1950–. (This and R.P.S.E. Shqiperise are the names currently used)
Sicilia, Bollo della Posta. SICILY.
Slesvig. SCHLESWIG. Plebiscite issues, 1920.
Slovensko/Slovanska Posta. SLOVAKIA.

Prussia

Saxony

Albania

Sweden

Sverige. SWEDEN.
Türkiye (or Turk) Postalari. TURKEY.
Türkiye Cumhuriyeti (or T.C.) Postalari. TURKEY.
Vallées d'Andorre. ANDORRA (French Post Offices), 1932–37.
Vaticane, Poste. VATICAN CITY.
Vereinte Nationen. UNITED NATIONS — Vienna Centre.
Württemberg. WURTTEMBERG. Independent Kingdom. Also GERMANY.
     Allied Occupation.
Zone Française. GERMANY French Zone. Allied Occupation, 1945–46.

B. Country Names: Rest of the World

Açores. AZORES.
Afghanes, Postes. AFGHANISTAN.
Africa Occidental Española. SPANISH WEST AFRICA.
Africa Orientale Italiana. ITALIAN EAST AFRICA.
Afrique Equatoriale Française. FRENCH EQUATORIAL AFRICA.
Afrique Occidentale Française. FRENCH WEST AFRICA.

Cambodia

French West Africa

Cape Verde Islands

Alexandrie. ALEXANDRIA. French Post Office.
Algérie. ALGERIA.
Archipel des Comores. COMORO ISLANDS.
Belgisch Congo. BELGIAN CONGO.
Benadir. SOMALIA, 1903–05.
Brasil. BRAZIL.
British Central Africa. NYASALAND PROTECTORATE, 1891–1903.
British New Guinea. Former name of PAPUA.
British South Africa Company. Former name of RHODESIA.
Brunei Darussalam. BRUNEI since 1984.
Cabo Verde. CAPE VERDE ISLANDS.
Cambodge. CAMBODIA.
Castellorizo/Catelloriso. CASTELROSSO. One of the Aegean Islands.
Cavalle. CAVALLA (KAVALLA). French Post Office.
Centrafricaine, République. CENTRAL AFRICAN REPUBLIC.
China, Republic of. CHINA, 1913–29 and CHINA (TAIWAN), 1953–.
Cilicie. CILICIA.
Cirenaica. CYRENAICA.
Comores, Archipel des. COMORO ISLANDS.
Congo Belge. BELGIAN CONGO.
Congo Français. FRENCH CONGO.
Congo Français Gabon. GABON.
Congo, République de. CONGO (Kinshasa), 1961–64; CONGO REPUBLIC
     (Brazzaville), 1959–70.
Congo, République Démocratique du. CONGO (Kinshasa), 1964–71.
Congo, République Populaire du. CONGO (Brazzaville), from 1970.

Somalia

Corée, Postes de. KOREA, 1902–03.

Côte d'Ivoire. IVORY COAST.

Côte Francais des Somalis. FRENCH SOMALI COAST.

Dansk Vestindiske Öer/Dansk Vestindien. DANISH WEST INDIES.

Datia. DUTTIA. A state of Central India.

Dédéagh. DEDEAGATZ.

Deutsch-Neu-Guinea. (GERMAN) NEW GUINEA.

Deutsch-Ostafrika. TANGANYIKA. Formerly German East Africa.

Deutsch-Sudwestafrika. SOUTH WEST AFRICA. Formerly a German colony.

Danish West Indies

Dominicana, Republica. DOMINICAN REPUBLIC.

DPR Korea. NORTH KOREA. Issues since 1980 (stamps inscribed DPR of Korea in 1976).

Estado da India. PORTUGUESE INDIA.

Etablissements Français dans l'Inde. INDIAN SETTLEMENTS.

Etablissements (or Ets.) Français de l'Océanie. OCEANIC SETTLEMENTS.

Etat Comorien. COMORO ISLANDS.

Etat Indépendant du Congo. BELGIAN CONGO. The former Congo Free State.

Ethiopie/Postes Ethiopiennes. ETHIOPIA.

Filipinas (or Filipas). PHILIPPINES. The former Spanish colony.

Grand Liban. LEBANON, 1924–26. 'Greater Lebanon'.

Grande Comore. GREAT COMORO.

Guiné. PORTUGUESE GUINEA.

Oceanic Settlements

Guinea Española. SPANISH GUINEA.

Guinea Ecuatorial, Republica de. EQUATORIAL GUINEA.

Guinée, also République de. GUINEA. The former French Guinea.

Guyane Française. FRENCH GUIANA.

Hadhramaut. ADEN PROTECTORATE STATE. Formerly Qu'aiti State of Shihr and Mukalla.

Haut (or Ht.) Sénégal-Niger. UPPER SENEGAL AND NIGER.

Haute-Volta. UPPER VOLTA.

Hejaz & Nejd. SAUDI ARABIA.

Holkar State. INDORE.

Ile de la Réunion. REUNION.

Portuguese Guinea

Iles Wallis et Futuna. WALLIS AND FUTUNA ISLANDS.

India/India Portugueza (or Port. or Portuguesa), Estadro da. PORTUGUESE INDIA.

Indo-Chine/Indochine. INDO-CHINA.

Irian Barat. WEST IRIAN. Formerly Netherlands New Guinea and West New Guinea.

Islas Galapagos. GALAPAGOS ISLANDS.

Jam. Dim. Soomaaliya. SOMALIA, 1974–75.

Jum. Dim. Somaliya. SOMALIA, 1973–74.

J.D. Soomaaliya. SOMALIA. 1976–77.

J.D. Soomaaliyeed. SOMALIA. 1977–.

Upper Volta

Kamerun. CAMEROUN. The former German colony.

Karolinen. CAROLINE ISLANDS. The former German proctectorate.

Kibris Türk Yönetimi/Kibris Türk Federe Devleti Postalari. TURKISH CYPRIOT POSTS.

Korea. SOUTH KOREA since 1980; **Republic of Korea,** 1961–64 and 1966–80.

(Postes) Lao. LAOS since 1976.

Liban/République Libanaise. LEBANON.

Macau. MACAO.

Mahra State. ADEN PROTECTORATE STATE.

Malgache, République/Malagasy, Repoblika. MALAGASY REPUBLIC. Formerly Madagascar.

Turkish Cypriot Posts

Maroc. FRENCH MOROCCO.
Maroc, Royaume du. MOROCCO. 'Kingdom of Morocco'.
Marruecos, etc. SPANISH MOROCCO.

Spanish Morocco

Mexico

Saudi Arabia

Mozambique

Malayan Federation

Marschall (or **Marshall**) **Inseln.** MARSHALL ISLANDS.
Mauritanie. MAURITANIA. West Africa.
Medellin. ANTIOQUIA (Colombia). Issue of 1888.
Mejico, Correos. MEXICO. Issues of 1856 and 1864.
Melaka Malaysia. MALACCA. Issues from 1965.
Moçambique. MOZAMBIQUE.
Moçambique, Companhia (or **Comp.**) **de.** MOZAMBIQUE COMPANY.
Moyen Congo. MIDDLE CONGO.
Nederlands (or **Ned.**) **Nieuw-Guinea.** NETHERLANDS NEW GUINEA.
Nederlandsch (**Ned.** or **Nederl**) **Indië.** NETHERLANDS INDIES.
Nederlandse (or **Ned.**) **Antillen.** NETHERLANDS ANTILLES.
Nieuwe Republiek. NEW REPUBLIC. South Africa.
Nippon. JAPAN.
Nouvelle (or **Nlle.**) **Caledonie et Dependances.** NEW CALEDONIA.
Nouvelles Hebrides, Condominium des. NEW HEBRIDES.
N. (**Negri** or **Negeri**) **Sembilan.** NEGRI SEMBILAN. Malaysia.
Océanie. OCEANIC SETTLEMENTS.
Oltre Giuba. JUBALAND.
Oranje Vrij Staat. ORANGE FREE STATE.
Oubangui-Chari/Oubangui-Chari-Tchad. UBANGI-SHARI. Central Africa.
Persanes, Postes. IRAN. Formerly 'Persia'.
Persekutuan Tanah Melayu. MALAYAN FEDERATION.
Pilipinas. PHILIPPINES.
Polynesie Francaise. FRENCH POLYNESIA.
Poste Khedivie e Giziane/Postes Egyptiennes. EGYPT, 1872–88.
Pto. Rico/Porto Rico (U.S.). PUERTO RICO.
Pulau Pinang Malaysia. PENANG. Issues from 1965.
Republica Oriental. URUGUAY.
Republic Khmere. KHMER REPUBLIC. Cambodia, 1971–74.
Royaume de l'Arabie Soudite (or **Saoudite**). SAUDI ARABIA.
Shihr and Mukalla. ADEN PROTECTORATE STATE. See 'Hadhramaut'.
Siam. THAILAND, 1887–1939.
Socialist People's Libyan Arab, Jamahiriya. LIBYA since 1977.
Soudan Français. FRENCH SUDAN.
Suidafrika (**Suid-Afrika** or **Republiek van Suid-Afrika**). SOUTH AFRICA.
Suidwes-Afrika. SOUTH WEST AFRICA.
Syrie/République Syrienne. SYRIA.

South West Africa

Tonga

Tunisia

Tchad. CHAD.

Terres Australes et Antarctiques Françaises. FRENCH SOUTHERN & ANTARCTIC TERRITORIES.

Territoire Français des Afars et des Issas. FRENCH TERRITORY OF THE AFARS AND THE ISSAS (formerly French Somali Coast).

Toga. TONGA, 1897–1944.

Togolaise, République. TOGO.

Touva. TUVA.

Transjordan. JORDAN.

Tunisie (or **République Tunisienne**). TUNISIA.

Van Diemen's Land. TASMANIA. First issues.

Western Samoa (or **Samoa i Sisifo**). SAMOA.

Zil Eloigne Sesel Seychelles. (Seychelles Outer Islands). ZIL ELWANNYEN SESEL.

Zil Elwagne Sesel Seychelles. *See above.*

Zuid Afrikaansche (or **Z. Afr.**) **Republiek.** TRANSVAAL.

Zuidwest Afrika. SOUTH WEST AFRICA.

C. Subordinate Inscriptions: Whole World

This section includes provisional overprints and surcharges, occupation issues and special-purpose inscriptions. Also see Abbreviations: Section D.

Admiralty Official. Overprint on British stamps 1903. GREAT BRITAIN— Official Stamps.

Africa. PORTUGUESE COLONIES, 1898. General issue.

Albania. With surcharge in para currency. ITALIAN P.O.s IN THE LEVANT.

Allemagne Duitschland. Belgian stamps overprinted for Rhineland. BELGIAN OCCUPATION OF GERMANY.

A.M. Post Deutschland. GERMANY. Allied Occupation—Anglo-American Zone, 1945.

Amtlicher Verkehr K. Württ. Post. WURTTEMBERG. Official Stamps.

Anna(s). Surcharged on British stamps. BRITISH POSTAL AGENCIES IN EASTERN ARABIA. Also on French stamps for FRENCH P.O.s IN ZANZIBAR.

A percevoir

Great Britain
Army Official

German Occupation

San Marino

A payer te betalen. BELGIUM. Postage dues.

A percevoir. 'To collect'. BELGIUM, FRANCE, GUADELOUPE, CANADA, EGYPT, MONACO. Postage dues.

A percevoir timbre taxe. FRENCH COLONIES. Postage dues.

Army Official. Overprint on British stamps 1896–1902. GREAT BRITAIN— Official Stamps. Also overprint on Sudan stamps. SUDAN—Army Service Stamps.

Army Service. Overprint on Sudan stamps, 1906. SUDAN—Army Service Stamps.

Assistência D.L. no.72. Educational Tax overprint. TIMOR, 1936–37.

Autopaketti. For parcels carried by road. FINLAND.

Avion Nessre Tafari. Airmail stamps. ETHIOPIA, 1931.

Avisporto Maerke. Newspaper stamps. DENMARK.

Bánát Bacska. Overprint on Hungarian stamps. RUMANIAN OCCUPATION OF HUNGARY.

Bani and lei. Surcharges for K.u.K.Feldpost. AUSTRO-HUNGARIAN MILITARY POST—Issues for Rumania.

Baranya. Overprint/surcharges on Hungarian stamps. SERBIAN OCCUPATION OF HUNGARY.

Belgien. Overprint/surcharges on German stamps. GERMAN OCCUPATION OF BELGIUM.

Bengasi. Overprint/surcharges on Italian stamps. ITALIAN P.O.s IN THE LEVANT.

Berlin. Overprint on Allied Occupation stamps (1947) for GERMANY—West Berlin.

Board of Education. Overprint on British stamps 1902. GREAT BRITAIN— Official Stamps.

Bollo Postale. 'Postage Stamp'. SAN MARINO, 1877–1935.

British Bechuanaland. Overprint and inscription. BECHUANALAND, 1885– 1891.

British Occupation. Overprint/surcharges on Russian and Batum stamps. BATUM, 1919–20.

British Somaliland. Overprint on Indian stamps for the SOMALILAND PROTECTORATE.

Buchanan. Registration stamp of LIBERIA 1893.

Bureau International d'Education. UNITED NATIONS (Geneva). International Education Office.

Bureau International du Travail. UNITED NATIONS (Geneva). International Labour Office.

Cabo Jubi/Cabo Juby. Overprint on stamps of Rio de Oro, Spain or Spanish Morocco. CAPE JUBY.

Calimno/Calino. Overprint on Italian stamps for Kalimnos. AEGEAN ISLANDS.

Carchi/Karki. Overprint on Italian stamps for Khalki. AEGEAN ISLANDS.

Cameroons U.K.T.T. Overprint on Nigerian stamps. SOUTHERN CAMEROONS—United Kingdom Trust Territory.

Caso. Overprint on Italian stamps for Kasos. AEGEAN ISLANDS.

Cefalonia e Itaca. Part of overprint on Greek stamps. CEPHALONIA AND ITHACA. Italian Occupation.

Cent. Also **F.** for franc. Surcharges for Belgium and Northern France. GERMAN COMMANDS.

Centesimi and lire. Surcharges for K.u.K. Feldpost. AUSTRO-HUNGARIAN MILITARY POST—Issues for Italy.

Centesimo (or centesimi) di corona. Surcharge on Italian stamps for ITALIAN AUSTRIA.

Centimes. Surcharge on German stamps for GERMAN P.O.s IN TURKEY. Also on stamps of Austria for AUSTRIAN P.O.s IN CRETE.

Centimos. Surcharge on French stamps for FRENCH P.O.s IN MOROCCO.

Chemins de Fer Spoorwegen. Railway Parcels stamps. BELGIUM.

Belgium. Railway
Parcels Stamp

China. Overprint on Hong Kong stamps for CHINA: BRITISH POST OFFICES. Also on German stamps for GERMAN P.O.s IN CHINA.

Chine. Overprint, surcharges and inscription for FRENCH P.O.s IN CHINA.

Cinquantenaire 24 Septembre 1853–1903 and eagle overprint on French stamps for 50th anniversary of French Occupation. NEW CALEDONIA.

Colombia. COLOMBIA. Also inscribed on stamps of PANAMA, 1887–92.

Coloniale Italiane, R.R. Poste. ITALIAN COLONIES. General issues, 1932–34.

Colonie Italiane. Overprint on Italian 'Dante' stamps of 1932 for ITALIAN COLONIES.

Colonies de l'Empire Français. FRENCH COLONIES. 'Eagle' issue, 1859.

Colonies Postes. FRENCH COLONIES. French 'Commerce' type, 1881. NOTE.—French stamps without special distinction or inscription were also issued for the French Colonies up to 1877. For details see under 'France' in the Catalogue.

Comité Francais de la Liberation Nationale. With R.F. or République Francaise. FRENCH COLONIES, 1943.

Confed. Granadina. COLOMBIA, 1859.

Congreso de los Diputados. SPAIN, Official stamps, 1895.

Constantinopol Posta Romana. Circular overprint on Rumanian stamps. RUMANIAN P.O.s ABROAD—Constantinople.

Constantinopoli. Overprint and surcharges on Italian stamps. ITALIAN P.O.s IN THE LEVANT. For Constantinople.

Corfu. Overprint and surcharges on Italian stamps. CORFU (Italian Occupation). Also overprint on Greek stamps. CORFU AND PAXOS (Italian Occupation).

Cos or Coo. Overprint on Italian stamps for Kos, AEGEAN ISLANDS.

Cour Internationale de Justice or Cour Permanente, etc. Overprint/inscription on special stamps for the Court of International Justice, The Hague. NETHERLANDS.

Courrier de la Societé des Nations. Overprint on Swiss stamps for the League of Nations. UNITED NATIONS (Geneva).

Courrier du Bureau International du Travail. Overprint on Swiss stamps for the International Labour Office. UNITED NATIONS (Geneva).

Courrier du Bureau International d'Education. Overprint on Swiss stamps for the International Education Office. UNITED NATIONS (Geneva).

Crete. Overprint and surcharges on French stamps. FRENCH P.O.s IN CRETE.

Deficit. Overprint/inscription on postage due stamps. PERU.

Demokratska Federativna Jugoslavija. Overprint/surcharges on Croatian stamps. YUGOSLAVIA (Democratic Federation). Regional issues.

Deutsche Feldpost. GERMANY. Military Fieldpost stamps, 1944.

Deutsche Flugpost/Deutsche Luftpost. GERMANY. Airmail stamps, 1919–38.

Deutsche Post Osten. Overprint and surcharges on German stamps for Nazi Occupation. POLAND, 1939.

Dienstmarke. GERMANY. Official stamps from 1920.

Diligencia. URUGUAY. 'Mailcoach' issue of 1856.

Dios Patria Libertad. DOMINICAN REPUBLIC. Inscription on early issues.

Durazzo. Overprint and surcharges on Italian stamps. ITALIAN P.O.s IN THE LEVANT.

East Africa and Uganda Protectorates. Listed under KENYA, UGANDA AND TANGANYIKA.

East India Postage. INDIA. Stamps of 1860. Also, surcharged with a crown and value in cents—STRAITS SETTLEMENTS first issue of 1867.

Egeo. Overprint on Italian stamps. AEGEAN ISLANDS, 1912.

Elsass. Overprint on German stamps. GERMAN OCCUPATION OF ALSACE.

Escuelas. 'Schools'. VENEZUELA. Fiscals valid for postal use.

Est Africain Allemand Occupation Belge or **Duitsch Oost Afrika Belgische**

KUT

Bezetting (Flemish). Overprint on Beligan Congo stamps for Belgian Occupation of RUANDA-URUNDI.

Estados Unidos de Nueva Granada. COLOMBIA, 1861.

Estensi, Poste. MODENA, 1852.

Estero. 'Foreign'. Overprint on modified Italian stamps for ITALIAN P.O.s IN THE LEVANT.

Estland Eesti. GERMAN OCCUPATION OF ESTONIA.

Eupen & Malmédy. Overprint/surcharges on Belgian stamps. BELGIAN OCCUPATION OF GERMANY.

Fiume Rijeka. Overprint with date 3-V-1945 and surcharges on Italian stamps. VENEZIA GIULIA AND ISTRIA. Yugoslav Occupation.

Florida. With picture of heron. URUGUAY. Air stamp of 1925.

Forces Françaises Libres Levant. Overprint and Lorraine Crosses/surcharges on Syrian and Lebanese stamps for FREE FRENCH FORCES IN THE LEVANT.

Franc. Surcharges on Austrian stamps. AUSTRIAN POST OFFICES IN CRETE.

Franco. 'Helvetia' seated. SWITZERLAND, 1854.

Franco Bollo. 'Postage stamp'. First issues of ITALY and SARDINIA. With 'Postale' added to crossed keys design: PAPAL STATES.

Papal States

Franco Marke. BREMEN, 1856.

Franco Scrisorei. RUMANIA, 1862.

Francobollo di Stato. ITALY. Official stamps.

Freimarke. 'Postage stamp'. With portrait, PRUSSIA, 1850. With large numerals, THURN AND TAXIS.

Frimaerke Kgl. Post or **Kgl. Post. Frm.** DENMARK/DANISH WEST INDIES. Kgl. or Kongeligt means 'Royal'.

General Gouvernement. Nazi Occupation of POLAND, 1940–44.

Gen.-Gouv. Warschau. Overprint on German stamps. GERMAN OCCUPATION OF POLAND.

Georgie (La) or **République Georgienne.** GEORGIA, 1919–21. Now part of the Soviet Union.

Denmark

Gerusalemme. Overprint and surcharges on Italian stamps for Jerusalem. ITALIAN P.O.s IN THE LEVANT.

Golfo de Guinea, Territorios (or Terrs.) del. Overprint on Spanish stamps for SPANISH GUINEA.

Govt. Parcels. Overprint on British stamps 1883–1902. GREAT BRITAIN — Official Stamps.

Granadina, Confed. COLOMBIA, 1859.

Grenville. Registration stamp of LIBERIA 1893.

Harper. Registration stamp of LIBERIA 1893.

H.E.H. The Nizam's Government/Silver Jubilee. HYDERABAD. Indian state.

Herzogth. (or Herzogthum) Holstein/Schleswig. SCHLESWIG-HOLSTEIN. Two former grand-duchies.

Hrvatska SHS. Overprint on Hungarian stamps for Croatia, 1918. YUGOSLAVIA.

Great Britain
Govt. Parcels

Ile Rouad. Overprint and surcharges on French stamps for ROUAD ISLAND (ARWAD).

Imperial British East Africa Company. BRITISH EAST AFRICA.

Impuesto (or Impto.) de Guerra. SPAIN. War Tax stamps.

Instruccion. 'Instruction' or 'Teaching'. VENEZUELA. Fiscals valid for postage.

I.R. Official. Overprint on British stamps 1882–1902. GREAT BRITAIN — Official Stamps (Inland Revenue).

Isole Italiani dell 'Egeo. Overprint on Italian stamps. AEGEAN ISLANDS.

Isole Jonie. Overprint on Italian stamps. IONIAN ISLANDS. Italian Occupation.

Istra. Overprint and surcharges on Italian stamps. VENEZIA GIULIA AND ISTRIA.

Ita-Karjala Sot. hallinto. Overprint on Finnish stamps. FINNISH OCCUPATION OF EASTERN KARELIA.

Janina. Overprint and surcharges on Italian stamps. ITALIAN P.O.s IN THE LEVANT.

Jeend (Jhind or **Jind) State.** Overprint on Indian stamps for JIND. Indian state.

Kalayaan nang Pilipinas. JAPANESE OCCUPATION OF PHILIPPINES.

Karki. Overprint on Italian stamps for Khalki. AEGEAN ISLANDS.

Karnten Abstimmung. Overprint on modified Austrian stamps. AUSTRIA. Carinthian plebiscite, 1920.

Keneta. 'Cent' or 'cents'. Elua keneta — 'Two cents' etc. HAWAII.

Kenttapostia Faltpost. FINLAND. Military Field Post.

K.K. Post-Stempel. 'Imperial/Royal Postage Stamp'. In kreuzer denominations — AUSTRIA first issue. In 'centes' — LOMBARDY AND VENETIA.

Austria

Klaipeda. Overprint, surcharges or inscription for MEMEL — Lithuanian Occupation.

K.u.K. Feldpost. 'Imperial and Royal Field Post'. AUSTRO-HUNGARIAN MILITARY POST.

K.u.K. Milit. Verwaltung Montenegro. Overprint on K.u.K. Feldpost stamps for the AUSTRO-HUNGARIAN MILITARY POST — Montenegro issues.

K.u.K. Militärpost. BOSNIA AND HERZEGOVINA. Austro-Hungarian Military Post.

La Canea. Overprint and surcharges on Italian stamps. ITALIAN P.O.s IN CRETE.

LANSA (Lineas Aereas Nacionales Sociedad Anonima). COLOMBIA. Private Air Companies.

Lattaquie. Overprint on Syrian stamps for LATAKIA (formerly Alaouites).

Latvija 1941·I·VII. Overprint on Russian stamps for GERMAN OCCUPATION OF LATVIA.

Latvijas Aizsargi. 'Latvian Militia'. Overprint and surcharges. LATVIA, 1931.

Latvijas PSR. LATVIA. Issue inscribed for absorption of Latvia by Soviet Union, 1940.

Lero or Leros. Overprint on Italian stamps for Leros. AEGEAN ISLANDS.

Levant. Overprint on British stamps for Middle East post offices. BRITISH LEVANT. Also overprint on Polish stamps for POLISH P.O. IN TURKEY.

Levante. Overprint and surcharges on Italian Express Letter stamps for ITALIAN P.O.s IN THE LEVANT.

Lignes Aeriennes F.A.F.L. Overprint and surcharges on Syrian air stamps of 1931. FREE FRENCH FORCES IN THE LEVANT, 1942.

Lima. Inscription and overprint on early issues of Peru (Lima is the capital).

Lipso or Lisso. Overprint on Italian stamps for Lipso. AEGEAN ISLANDS.

Lösen. Inscription on postage due stamps for SWEDEN, 1874.

Peru

Lothringen. Overprint on German stamps for GERMAN OCCUPATION OF LORRAINE, 1940.

Lubiana, R. Commissariato Civile etc. Overprint of Yugoslav stamps for the Italian Occupation of SLOVENIA.

Luftfeldpost. Inscription of Nazi air stamp of 1942. GERMANY — Military Fieldpost.

Mafia, G.R.Post. Overprint on Indian Expeditionary Force stamps for TANGANYIKA — British Occupation, 1915.

Malmédy. See Eupen & Malmédy.

Marianen. Inscription and overprint on German stamps for the MARIANA ISLANDS.

Marocco or Marokko. Overprint and surcharges on German stamps for GERMAN P.O.s IN MOROCCO.

Memelgebiet. Overprint and surcharges on German stamps for MEMEL.

Milliemes/Mill. Surcharges on French Colonial stamps. ALEXANDRIA and PORT SAID.

Monrovia. Registration stamp of LIBERIA 1893.

Nationaler Verwaltungsausschus 10·XI·1943. Overprint on Italian Occupation stamps for MONTENEGRO—German Occupation.

Nepriklausoma Lietuva 1941·VI·23. Overprint on Russian stamps for GERMAN OCCUPATION OF LITHUANIA.

Nezavisna Drzava (or N.D.) Hrvatska. Inscription or overprint on Yugoslav stamps for CROATIA.

Nisiro or Nisiros. Overprint on Italian stamps for Nisiros. AEGEAN ISLANDS.

Nlle. Caledonie. Inscription or overprint on French stamps. NEW CALEDONIA.

Nueva Granada, etc. See Estados Unidos.

Occupation Française. Overprint and surcharges on Hungarian stamps for FRENCH OCCUPATION OF HUNGARY—Arad.

O.F. Castelloriso. 'Occupation Francaise'. Overprint on French stamps for Occupation of CASTELROSSO.

Offentlig Sak/Off. Sak./O.S. Official stamps of NORWAY.

Oil Rivers, British Protectorate. Overprint/surcharges on British stamps for Oil Rivers Protectorate. NIGER COAST PROTECTORATE.

O.M.F. Cilicie. 'Occupation Militaire Francaise'. Overprint/surcharges on French stamps for French Military Occupation of CILICIA. Also on Turkish fiscal stamps.

O.M.F. Syrie. 'Occupation Militaire Francaise'. Overprint/surcharges on French stamps for French Military Occupation of SYRIA.

O.N.F. (or B.N.F.) Castellorizo. 'Occupation (or Base) Navale Francaise'. Overprint/surcharges on French/French Levant stamps for French Occupation of CASTELROSSO.

Orange River Colony. Overprint on Cape of Good Hope stamps, or inscription, for former ORANGE FREE STATE (South Africa).

Ostland. Overprint on German stamps for GERMAN OCCUPATION OF RUSSIA, 1941.

O.W. Official. Overprint on British stamps 1896–1902. GREAT BRITAIN-Official Stamps (Office of Works).

Pacchi Postali. 'Parcel Post'. ITALY. Also, inscribed 'R.S. Marino', SAN MARINO.

Italy

Packhoi. Overprint and Chinese surcharges on Indo-Chinese stamps for PAKHOI.

Pakke-Porto. 'Parcel Post'. GREENLAND.

Para(s). Currency inscription on first issues of EGYPT. Also surcharges on stamps for AUSTRIAN P.O.s IN TURKEY, BRITISH LEVANT, FRENCH LEVANT, GERMAN P.O.s IN TURKEY, ITALIAN P.O.s IN THE LEVANT, RUMANIAN P.O.s ABROAD, RUSSIAN P.O.s IN TURKEY.

Parlamento a Cervantes, El. Cervantes commemorative. Official stamps of SPAIN, 1916.

Patmo or Patmos. Overprint on Italian stamps for Patmos. AEGEAN ISLANDS.

Pechino. Overprint/surcharges on Italian stamps for Peking. ITALIAN P.O.s IN CHINA.

Pentru Cultura. Inscription on Postal Tax stamps of RUMANIA 1932.

Pesa. Surcharges on German stamps for German East Africa. TANGANYIKA.

Peseta(s). Surcharges on French stamps for FRENCH P.O.s IN MOROCCO.

Piaster. Surcharges on Austrian stamps for AUSTRIAN P.O.s IN TURKEY. Also on German stamps for GERMAN P.O.s IN TURKEY.

Piastre(s). Surcharges on stamps for BRITISH LEVANT, FRENCH LEVANT, ITALIAN P.O.s IN THE LEVANT, RUSSIAN P.O.s IN TURKEY.

Piscopi. Overprint on Italian stamps for Tilos (Piskopi). AEGEAN ISLANDS.

Plebiscite Olsztyn Allenstein. Overprint on German stamps for plebiscite in ALLENSTEIN, 1920.

Port Gdansk. Overprint on Polish stamps for POLISH POST IN DANZIG.

Porte Franco. Inscription on early issues of PERU.

Porteado Correio. Postage Due stamps of PORTUGAL.

Porto Gazetei (Moldavian 'Bulls') or **Porto Scrisorei.** Earliest issues of RUMANIA.

Rumania
(Moldavia)

Porto Rico. Overprint on U.S. stamps for Military Occupation of PUERTO RICO.

Portzegel. Overprint and surcharges for Postage Dues. NETHERLANDS.

Post & Receipt or **Post Stamp.** Inscriptions on 'annas' stamps of HYDERABAD.

Postzegel. Inscription on first issues of NETHERLANDS.

Pro Juventute. 'For the Children'. Charity stamps of SWITZERLAND.

Pro Patria. 'For the Fatherland'. National culture fund stamps of SWITZERLAND.

Protectorado Español en Marruecos. SPANISH MOROCCO.

Protectorat Français. Overprint on French 'Maroc' key-types for FRENCH MOROCCO.

Provinz Laibach/Ljubljanska Pokrajina. Inscription/overprints on Italian stamps for German Occupation of SLOVENIA.

Puolustusvoimat Kenttäpostia. FINLAND. Military Field Post.

Puttialla State. Overprint on Indian stamps for first issues of PATIALA.

Switzerland

Rarotonga. Overprint/surcharges on New Zealand stamps, also inscription. COOK ISLANDS.

Recargo/Recargo Transitorio de Guerra. SPAIN. War Tax stamps.

Regatul Romaniei. Overprints with values in bani, leu or lei on Hungarian stamps for RUMANIA — Transylvania, 1919.

Regno d'Italia Trentino 3 nov 1918/Venezia Giulia 3·XI·18. Overprints on Austrian stamps for ITALIAN AUSTRIA.

Retymno. Rethymnon Province — RUSSIAN POST OFFICES IN CRETE.

R.H. Official. Royal Household. GREAT BRITAIN — Official stamps.

Rialtar Sealadac na Heireann 1922. 'Provisional Government of Ireland'. Overprint on British stamps for IRELAND (REPUBLIC).

Robertsport. Registration stamp of LIBERIA 1893.

Rodi. Overprints on Italian stamps, or inscription, for Rhodes. AEGEAN ISLANDS.

Roumelie Orientale or **R.O.** Overprint on Turkish stamps, or inscription, for EASTERN ROUMELIA (SOUTH BULGARIA).

Rumänien. Overprint and value in 'bani' surcharged on German stamps. GERMAN OCCUPATION OF RUMANIA.

Rupee(s). Surcharges on British stamps for BRITISH POSTAL AGENCIES IN EASTERN ARABIA.

Russisch-Polen. Overprint on German stamps for GERMAN OCCUPATION OF POLAND.

S. Thomé (or **Tomé**) **e Principe.** ST. THOMAS AND PRINCE ISLANDS.

Salonicco. Overprint and surcharges on Italian stamps for Salonika (Thessaloniki). ITALIAN P.O.s IN THE LEVANT.

Sandjak d'Alexandrette. Overprint/surcharges on Syrian stamps. HATAY.

St. Thomas and
Prince Islands

Italy

Ireland

Saorstát Eireann 1922. 'Irish Free State'. Overprint on British stamps for IRELAND (REPUBLIC).

Saurashtra. SORUTH. (Indian state).

Scarpanto. Overprint on Italian stamps for Karpathos. AEGEAN ISLANDS.

Scutari di Albania. Overprint/surcharges on Italian stamps for ITALIAN P.O.s IN THE LEVANT.

Segnatasse. ITALY. Postage Due stamps.

Serbien. Overprint/surcharges on Yugoslav stamps for German Occupation of SERBIA; also overprint on Bosnian stamps for Serbian Issues of AUSTRO-HUNGARIAN MILITARY POST.

Shanghai China. Overprint/surcharges on U.S. stamps for UNITED STATES POSTAL AGENCY IN SHANGHAI.

Simi. Overprint on Italian stamps for Simi. AEGEAN ISLANDS.

Smirne. Overprint/surcharges on Italian stamps for Smyrna (Izmir). ITALIAN P.O.s IN THE LEVANT.

Sowjetische Besatszungs Zone. Overprint on German stamps for GERMANY Allied Occupation, Russian Zone.

Stampalia. Overprint on Italian stamps for Astipalaia. AEGEAN ISLANDS.

Sud Kasai, Etat Autonome du. Overprint and inscription. SOUTH KASAI.

Tanger. Overprint on French/French Morocco stamps for FRENCH P.O.s in TANGIER; Also on Spanish stamps for SPANISH MOROCCO—TANGIER.

Morocco Agencies

Tangier. Overprint on British stamps for MOROCCO AGENCIES—Tangier International Zone.

Taxa de Guerra. War Tax surcharge. PORTUGUESE COLONIES/ GUINEA/INDIA, MACAO. Distinguished by currencies.

Te Betalen Port. Postage Due stamps of NETHERLANDS, CURACAO, SURINAM.

Territorios Espanoles del Golfo de Guinea. Inscription or overprint on Spanish stamps for SPANISH GUINEA.

Tetuan. Handstamp on Spanish stamps for SPANISH MOROCCO—Spanish P.O.s in Morocco.

Thirty Two Cents. With sailing ship. LIBERIA, 1886.

Tientsin. Overprint/surcharges on Italian stamps for ITALIAN P.O.s IN CHINA.

Tjeneste Frimaerke. Official stamps of DENMARK.

Tjenestefrimerke. Official stamps of NORWAY. First issue, 1925.

Toscano, Francobollo Postale. TUSCANY.

Tripoli di Barberia. Overprint on Italian stamps for ITALIAN P.O.s IN THE LEVANT.

Ukraine. Overprint on German stamps for GERMAN OCCUPATION OF RUSSIA, 1941.

Ultramar. 'Beyond the Seas'. Inscription with year dates on stamps of CUBA, also overprinted for PUERTO RICO. Appears also on postal-fiscals of MACAO and PORTUGUESE GUINEA.

Valona. Overprint/surcharges on Italian stamps for VALONA (Vlonë). ITALIAN P.O.s IN THE LEVANT.

Venezia Giulia/Tridentina (Trentino). Overprint/surcharges on Italian stamps for ITALIAN AUSTRIA.

Vilnius. Overprint on Russian stamps for GERMAN OCCUPATION OF LITHUANIA.

Virgin Islands. BRITISH VIRGIN ISLANDS.

Vojna Uprava Jugoslavenske Armije. Overprint/surcharges on Yugoslav stamps for VENEZIA GIULIA AND ISTRIA — Yugoslav Military Government.

Vom Empfänger Einzuziehen/Zahlbar. Inscriptions on DANZIG/BAVARIA. Postage Dues.

Wendenschen Kreises, Briefmarke des/Packenmarke des. WENDEN.

Yunnansen/Yunnanfou. Overprint/surcharges on Indo-Chinese stamps. YUNNANFU.

Zanzibar. Overprint/surcharges on French stamps for FRENCH P.O.s IN ZANZIBAR.

Zona de Ocupatie Romana in small oval. Overprint on Hungarian stamps for Debrecen. RUMANIAN OCCUPATION OF HUNGARY.

Zona Occupata Fiumano Kupa. Overprint on Yugoslav stamps for FIUME AND KUPA ZONE.

Zona (de) Protectorado Español/en Marruecos. SPANISH MOROCCO.

D. Abbreviations on Stamps: Whole World

A. Overprint for Avianca Air Company. COLOMBIA.

A & T. Overprint/surcharges on French Colonies 'Commerce' stamps for ANNAM AND TONGKING.

A.E.F. 'Afrique Equatoriale Francaise'. FRENCH EQUATORIAL AFRICA. 'Centenaire du Gabon' issue of 1938.

A.M.G.F.T.T. 'Allied Military Government — Free Territory of Trieste'. Overprint on Italian stamps. TRIESTE.

A.M.G.V.G. 'Allied Military Government — Venezia Giulia'. Overprint on Italian stamps. VENEZIA GIULIA AND ISTRIA.

Colombia

A.O. 'Afrique Orientale'. Overprint on Belgian Congo Red Cross stamps for Belgian Occupation of RUANDA-URUNDI.

B. 'Bangkok'. Overprint on Straits Settlements stamps for British Post Office in BANGKOK (Siam/Thailand).

B. Within oval. Overprint and inscription on Railway Official stamps of BELGIUM.

B.C.A. Overprint on Rhodesian stamps for British Central Africa Protectorate. NYASALAND PROTECTORATE.

B.C.O.F. JAPAN 1946. 'British Commonwealth Occupation Forces'. Overprint on Australian stamps. BRITISH OCCUPATION OF JAPAN.

B.I.E. Overprint on Swiss stamp for the Bureau International d'Education, 1946. UNITED NATIONS — International Education Office.

India (China Expeditionary Force)

BMA MALAYA. Overprint on Straits Settlements stamps. MALAYA — British Military Administration.

BMA (or BA) SOMALIA. Overprints/surcharges on British stamps. SOMALIA.

C.E.F. Overprint on Indian stamps for CHINA EXPEDITIONARY FORCE; also with surcharges on German 'Kamerun' stamps for Cameroons Expeditionary Force. CAMEROUN — British Occupation of Cameroons.

CFA. 'Communauté Financielle Africaine'. Overprint/surcharges on French stamps for REUNION.

C.G.H.S. Overprint on German Official stamps for plebiscite in UPPER SILESIA.

Co. Ci. 'Commissariato Civile'. Overprint on Yugoslav stamps for the Italian Occupation of SLOVENIA.

D de A. 'Departmento de Antioquia'. Inscription on issue of 1890. ANTIOQUIA.

Kamerun (Cameroons Expeditionary Force)

East Germany

Saudi Arabia showing
only Palm Tree

Libya

DDR. 'Deutsches Demokratische Republik'. (German Democratic Republic). Listed under GERMANY—East Germany.

DJ. Overpint on Obock stamp for DJIBOUTI, 1893.

D.P.R.K. Democratic People's Republic of Korea. NORTH KOREA, 1977–80.

E.A.F. 'East African Forces'. Overprint on British stamps for SOMALIA—British Occupation, 1943–46.

E.E.F. 'Egyptian Expeditionary Force'. Inscription on stamps of PALESTINE, 1918–22.

E.R.I. 6d. Overprint/surcharge on 6d. stamp of ORANGE FREE STATE, 1902.

G. Overprint on Cape of Good Hope stamps for GRIQUALAND WEST, 1877.

G et D (or G & D). Overprint/surcharges on Guadeloupe stamps for Guadeloupe and Dependencies. GUADELOUPE.

GAB. Overprint and surcharges on French Colonial stamp for GABON, 1886.

G.E.A. 'German East Africa'. Overprint on Kenya and Uganda stamps for British Occupation of TANGANYIKA.

G.F.B. 'Gaue Faka Buleaga' (On Government Service). Overprint on Tonga stamps, 1893. TONGA—Official Stamps.

G.K.C.A. Within dotted circle. Overprint/surcharges on Yugoslav stamps for the Carinthian plebiscite, 1920. YUGOSLAVIA.

G.P.E. Overprint/surcharges on French Colonies stamps for GUADELOUPE.

G.R.I. 'Georgius Rex Imperator'. Overprint and surcharges in British currency on stamps and registration labels of German New Guinea and Marshall Islands during Australian Occupation of NEW GUINEA; also on German Cameroons stamps for New Zealand administration of SAMOA.

G.W. Overprint on Cape of Good Hope stamps for GRIQUALAND WEST, 1877.

H.I. Postage. 'Hawaiian Islands'. HAWAII.

I.B. 'Irian Barat'. WEST IRIAN. Now part of Indonesia.

I.E.F. Overprint on Indian stamps for INDIAN EXPEDITIONARY FORCES.

I.E.F.'D'. Overprint/surcharges in annas for Indian forces in Mesopotamia. MOSUL. on Turkish fiscal stamps.

Kgl. Post. Frm. See 'Frimaerke Kgl. Post, Section C.

K.K., K.u.K. etc. See Section C.

K.S.A. Kingdom of SAUDI ARABIA. Stamps so inscribed 1975–82, since when inscription in Arabic only. Stamps identifiable by palm tree and crossed swords emblem.

L. Marques. Overpring on Mozambique stamps for LOURENCO MARQUES.

L.A.R. 'Libyan Arab Republic'. LIBYA, 1969–77.

M.E.F. Overprint on British stamps for British Forces in former Italian colonies. MIDDLE EAST FORCES.

M.V.i.R. Within frame. 'Militärverwaltung in Rumänien' ('Military Administration in Rumania'). Overprint/surcharges in 'bani' on German stamps for the GERMAN OCCUPATION OF RUMANIA.

N.C.E. or N.-C.E. Overprint/surcharges on French Colonies stamps for NEW CALEDONIA.

N.F. Overprint on Nyasaland stamps for Nyasa-Rhodesian Force during British Occupation of TANGANYIKA, 1916. Sometimes erroneously ascribed to '(Gen.) Northey's Force'.

NP. 'Naye paise' (Indian currency). Surcharges on British stamps for BRITISH POSTAL AGENCIES IN EASTERN ARABIA.

NSB. Overprint/surcharges on French Colonies stamps for NOSSI-BE (Madagascar).

N.S.W. NEW SOUTH WALES.

N.W. Pacific Islands. 'North-West Pacific Islands'. Overprint on Australian stamps for NEW GUINEA.

O.S. Overprint on Australian stamps. AUSTRALIA — Official Stamps. Also see 'Offentlig Sak' etc. in Section C.

O.S.G.S. 'On Sudan Government Service'. Overprint on Sudanese stamps. SUDAN — Official Stamps.

P.G.S. 'Perak Government Service'. Overprint on Straits Settlements stamps. PERAK — Official Stamps.

R. Overprint/surcharges on French Colonies stamps for REUNION, 1885.

R.F. 'République Francaise'. FRANCE.

Sudan

France

South West Africa

R.H. 'Republique d'Haiti'. Abbreviation on Postage Due stamps. HAITI, 1898.

RSA. 'Republic of South Africa'. SOUTH AFRICA.

R.S.M. 'Repubblica di San Marino'. SAN MARINO.

S. Overprint on Straits Settlements 2c. stamp for SELANGOR, 1882.

S.G. 'Sudan Government'. Overprint on Sudanese stamps. SUDAN — Official Stamps.

S.H.S. 'Srba (Serbs), Hrvata (Croats), Slovena (Slovenes)'. Early issues of YUGOSLAVIA.

S.O. 1920. Overprints on Czech and Polish stamps for EAST SILESIA (Silésie Orientale).

SPM or **St-Pierre M-on.** Overprint/surcharges on French Colonies stamps for ST. PIERRE ET MIQUELON.

S.T. Trsta Vuja. Yugoslav Military Government. TRIESTE.

STT Vuja (or **Vujna**). Overprints on Yugoslav stamps, 1949–54, for Zone B — Yugoslav Military Government. TRIESTE.

S.W.A. (or *SWA*). Overprints on South African stamps, also abbreviated inscription on stamps, for SOUTH WEST AFRICA.

T.E.O. 'Territoires Ennemis Occupés'. Overprint with surcharges in milliemes or piastres on French stamps for French Military Occupation of SYRIA. Also in paras on French Levant stamps for CILICIA.

T.E.O. Cilicie. Overprint on Turkish stamps for French Occupation of CILICIA.

U.A.R. 'United Arab Republic'. Inscription on various issues of Egypt and Syria from 1958.

U.G. Inscription on first 'Missionary' typewritten stamps for UGANDA, 1895.

UNEF. Overprint on Indian stamp for INDIAN U.N. FORCE IN GAZA (PALESTINE).

UNTEA. 'United Nations Temporary Executive Authority'. Overprint on stamps of Netherlands New Guinea for WEST NEW GUINEA.

U.S. UNITED STATES OF AMERICA.

U.S.S.R. 'Union of Soviet Socialist Republics'. RUSSIA.

V.R.I. 'Victoria Regina Imperatrix'. Overprint with values in British currency on Orange Free State stamps for British Occupation of ORANGE FREE STATE.

Y.A.R. YEMEN ARAB REPUBLIC.

United Arab Republic

Orange Free State

OTHER ALPHABETS AND SCRIPTS
A. The Cyrillic Group

Cyril and his brother Methodius were 9th-century saints, apostles of the Slavs and natives of Salonika (now Thessalonica). They worked as Christian missionaries among the Slav peoples, and it was in an effort to unify the Slavonic languages that Cyril, nicknamed 'the philosopher', created what became known as the Cyrillic alphabet, a modification of the Greek alphabet with marked individual characteristics, comprising 33 letters. Cyril set down his 'new' alphabet in AD 855, and it can be seen in the following tables that several Cyrillic characters are identical to those of the Greek alphabet: some indeed have the same English equivalents.

Despite these similarities the Cyrillic letters are really quite distinctive and once you have familiarized yourself with the Cyrillic alphabet tabled below, you will be able to recognize a stamp's country name or inscription at sight. You will then know that the stamp belongs to Russia (or one of its former districts or regional governments and post offices) and possibly Mongolia, to Yugoslavia (including the ancient kingdoms of Montenegro and Serbia), or to Bulgaria, which was once the territory of a great empire.

SIMPLIFIED CYRILLIC TABLE
with Russian-English equivalents

RUSSIA

The language of the peoples of Central Russia—which is also the official and literary language of the Russian nation—has a great many dialects, but in the main these are phonetic variations. The basic Cyrillic alphabet is universal throughout the country. Prior to the Revolution of 1917, Russian stamps were simply inscribed *mapka*, which translates as 'marka' or 'stamp', or with a word which looks like *noyta*, meaning 'pochta' or 'post'. Clues to identification are also provided by the currency denominations—the word which looks like *kon* is easily decoded as 'kop', short for 'kopeck', the unit of Russian currency. A hundred kopecks equal one 'rouble', a word which again is abbreviated on Russian stamps—the word, which looks like *pye*, is decoded as 'roob' or 'rouble'. Immediately following the Revolution, Russian stamps bore an inscription which looked something like 'P.C.I.C.P.'. This in interpreted as 'R.S.F.S.R.', an abbreviation for the provisional country name of 'Russian Socialist Federal Soviet Republic'. Since 1923 Russian stamps have been incribed *CCCP*, which translates as 'SSSR', the initial letters for the four Russian words meaning 'Union of Soviet Socialist Republics' (*Soyuz Sovyetskikh Sotsialisticheskikh Respublik*), familiar to us as 'U.S.S.R.'. Also familiar on modern Russian stamps is the word *noyta* which we now know means 'post'.

Stamps were issued in *Batum* (or Batoum), a town in Georgia on the eastern shore of the Black Sea, in 1919 during the British occupation following the War of 1914–18—the inscription in the scroll at the top of the stamps translates to *Batoomskaya pochta*, which means 'Batum post'. Stamps issued for the **Russian Post Offices in Turkey** in 1868 and 1879 can be identified by the inscription around the value numeral which may be decoded as *Vostochnaya korrespondentsia* or 'Oriental correspondence'. The penultimate letter 'I' in this inscription is now obsolete.

Simplified Decipherment Table

Russian Printed	'Handwritten'	English	Russian Printed	'Handwritten'	English
А а	*А а*	A	П п	*П п*	P
Б б	*Б б*	B	Р р	*Р р*	R
В в	*В в*	V	С с	*С с*	S
Г г	*Г г*	G	Т т	*Т т*	T
Д д	*Д д*	D	У у	*У у*	OO
Е е	*Е е*	E	Ф ф	*Ф ф*	F
Ё ё	*Ё ё*	YO	Х х	*Х х*	KH
Ж ж	*Ж ж*	ZH	Ц ц	*Ц ц*	TS
З з	*З з*	Z	Ч ч	*Ч ч*	CH
И и	*И и*	I	Ш ш	*Ш ш*	SH
Й й	*Й й*	I	Щ щ	*Щ щ*	SHCH
К к	*К к*	K	Ъ ъ	*Ъ ъ*	(silent)
Л л	*Л л*	L	Ы ы	*Ы ы*	I
М м	*М м*	M	Ь ь	*Ь ь*	(silent)
Н н	*Н н*	N	Э э	*Э э*	E
О о	*О о*	O	Ю ю	*Ю ю*	YU
			Я я	*Я я*	YA

Other Cyrillic Letters

Obsolete	I	і	I	*Serbian and*	J	j	J
	Ѣ	ѣ	YE	*Macedonian*	Љ	љ	LJ
	Ѳ	ѳ	F		Њ	њ	NJ
	Ѵ	ѵ	I		Џ	џ	DZ
	Ꙗ	ꙗ	U	*Mongolian*	Ү	ү	Ü
Ukrainian	Є	є	YE		Ѳ	ө	Ö*
Macedonian	Ѕ	ѕ	DZ				
Serbian	Ђ	ђ	DJ				
	Ћ	ћ	C	*Obsolete letter revived with new sound*			

Various anti-Bolshevik governments existed in **Siberia** for some years after the Revolution—the Cyrillic inscriptions and overprints are similar to those on Russian stamps and positive identification is best obtained by reference to the catalogue. **South Russia** also had temporary post-Revolution governments and here again reference to the catalogue illustrations is advised.

The **Ukraine** is a vast territory of the U.S.S.R. which issued stamps during its temporary independence after the Revolution, between 1918 and 1923. The 'trident' emblem on overprints and in designs is a clue to identity, while reference to the Cyrillic chart decodes the main inscription as *Ookrains'ka*, or Ukraine. For **West Ukraine**, Austrian stamps were overprinted with a trident in 1919 and letters which translate to *Z.Oo.N.R.*, meaning 'West Ukraine People's Republic'. **Wenden**, the 'Land of the Wends', now part of Latvia (the Latvian Soviet Republic), issued its own stamps up to 1901—the principal word in the inscription emerges as *Vendenskaya*. Earlier issues are inscribed in German—*Wendensche Kreis Briefmarke*.

Russian stamps were overprinted/surcharged for **Armenia**—mostly new-value surcharges and distinctive monogram devices; **Georgia**—surcharges, including the hammer and sickle, in 1923; and for the **Russian Post Offices in China**—note that the overprinted country name (which looks like the Greek name for 'Crete'), which translates as *Kitai*, is the Russian word for 'China'. **Mongolia**, the republic in Central Asia located between Russia and China, is largely under Russian influence. The Mongolian language used to be written in a vertical script and this is found on early stamps: then the Cyrillic alphabet was introduced on stamps in 1943 and has continued since. The common inscription translates as *Mongol shoodan*, or 'Mongolian post', while the Cyrillic initials *BNMAU* stand for 'All-in-agreement Mongol People's Country'. Mongolian stamps from 1959 have been additionally inscribed 'Mongolia' in the normal alphabet, thus making identification an easy matter.

Mongol shoodan   Montenegro

YUGOSLAVIA

The Socialist Federal Republic of Yugoslavia—the land of the southern Slavs—was proclaimed in 1945. It was however established in 1918 as the kingdom of the Serbs, Croats and Slovenes, comprising Montenegro, Serbia, Bosnia, Herzegovina and parts of pre-war Hungary, with separate stamp issues for the various states. In 1931, when the new country title of 'Jugoslavija' was officially adopted, definitive stamps appeared inscribed in Serbo-Croat (the *lingua franca* of Yugoslavia) and in the Cyrillic alphabet. Occasionally, since that time, Yugoslav stamps have been issued bearing only the Cyrillic inscription, but these are readily identifiable on reference to any of the dual-language stamps.

The former monarchy of **Montenegro** issued its own stamps from 1874 until 1913, and the country name—in Cyrillic characters—is rather misleading. It decodes in the native tongue as *Tsrna* (or *Tsr.*) *Gora*, or *Tsrne Gore*—in modern parlance, *Grna Gora*, in other words, Montenegro or 'Black Mountain'. *Poshte* is another version of the word for 'post'. The former kingdom of **Serbia** first issued stamps in 1866 and used the Cyrillic alphabet consistently, even through the German occupation of 1941–43. The country name is readily translatable as *Srbija*, *Srbska* or *Srpska*. Note that the 'j' is one of the Serbian special letters. The word for 'post' is *poshta*, and the currency is another clue—100 para equalling 1 dinar. The Cyrillic for 'para' looks like *napa*.

Srbija Poshta (Serbia)

BULGARIA

A Balkan republic, Bulgaria adjoins the Black Sea on the east, and is bounded by Rumania, Yugoslavia, Greece and Turkey. Formerly a Turkish province, it became a principality under Turkish suzerainty in 1878, while Eastern Roumelia was incorporated with it in 1885. Bulgaria's first stamps were issued in 1879, establishing the country name in Cyrillic letters which can be deduced as 'B'lgariya' (the second letter is silent and is thus represented by an apostrophe). With the accession of Tsar Ferdinand in 1907, the word for 'kingdom'—'Tsarstvo'—was introduced on subsequent stamps. The currency—100 stotinki = 1 lev (plural, leva)—is also easily identified: 'stotinki' is expressed as 'ctot. . . .'. After Bulgaria had become a republic in 1946, her stamps bore the Cyrillic letters 'HP' before the country name, translated as 'NR' or 'Narodna Republika' or 'People's Republic'. Modern Bulgarian stamps are sometimes inscribed 'NR Bulgaria' in the normal alphabet.

Bulgaria

B. *The Greek Alphabet*

Greek is one of the classic languages—its alphabet was 'borrowed' from the Phoenicians whose extinct Semitic language was allied to Carthaginian and akin to Hebrew, and was, perhaps, the first tongue written in an alphabet proper. The word 'alphabet' itself is derived from *alpha*, *beta*, the first two Greek letters. Greek stamps have the country name 'Hellas' expressed (in Greek) in a word which can be spelled out from the table below as *Ellas*. In fact since 1966 the version 'Hellas' has been printed alongside the Greek characters on the stamps.

SIMPLIFIED GREEK TABLE
with Greek-English equivalents

Greek	English	Greek	English
		N, ν	N
A, α	A	Ξ, ξ	X
B, β	B	O, o	O
Γ, γ	G	Π, π	P
Δ, δ	D	P, ρ	R
E, ε	E	Σ, σ	S
Z, ʒ	Z	ς (final)	
H, η	E	T, τ	T
Θ, θ	TH	Y, υ	U
I, ι	I	Φ, φ	F
K, κ	K	X, χ	KH
Λ, λ	L	Ψ, ψ	PS
M, μ	M	Ω, ω	O

Conventional English equivalents are given. The actual pronunciation of some letters differs in modern spoken Greek.

Look out for the distinctive currency inscription—100 *lepta* = 1 *drachma*. *Lepta* (singular, *lepton*) is expressed in a word which looks like 'AENTA' (although the first letter is an inverted 'V'), while *drachmai* (plural) appears at first glance as 'APAXMAI', though again the first letter is a triangle, the equivalent for 'D'. Sometimes these words are abbreviated. You may encounter overprints on Greek stamps and once you have decoded them it should be an easy matter to locate them in the catalogue. *Ellenike Dioikesis* ('Greek Administration') may be found on the Greek stamps of 1912 (provisionals for Balkan territories), or the Greek Occupation of Albania in 1940. The initials *S.D.D.* adjoining a surcharge within a scroll can be pinpointed to the Greek Occupation of the Dodecanese Islands. Thrace suffered various occupations in 1920, and a typical overprint reads, when decoded, *Dioikesis Dutikes Frakes* or 'Administration of Western Thrace'. Stamps for the Greek island for Crete bear an inscription which translates as *Krete*.

C. Indian Native States

Prior to independence in 1947, India embraced numerous princely states, some of which issued stamps. For convenience, philatelists divide them into two groups—the so-called Convention States and the Indian Feudatory States. The Convention States, which, under a series of postal conventions established by the Imperial Government, used Indian stamps overprinted with their various names (usually in English and thus easily identified), were: Chamba; Faridkot after 1887; Gwalior; Jind (Jhind or Jeend) from 1885; Nabha; and Patiala (also spelled Puttialla). The exceptional overprint of Gwalior official stamps is illustrated. These stamps were valid for postage within the state of issue, to other Convention states and to destinations in British India.

Stamps in a wide variety of often primitive designs were issued by the Indian Feudatory States—these could only be used within the borders of their respective states. Some issues are extremely rare and the whole group has become quite popular with collectors seeking a novel and complex subject for philatelic study. Some typical designs are illustrated from each Feudatory State. With the exception of the 'Anchal' stamps of Travancore-Cochin (1951), all these stamps were replaced by those of the Republic of India on 1 May 1950.

INDIAN FEUDATORY STATES

Alwar

Bahawalpur

Bamra

Barwani

Bhopal

Bhor

Bijawar

Bundi

Bussahir

Charkhari

Cochin

Dhar

Duttia

Faridkot pre-1887

Hyderabad

Idar

Indore (Holkar)

Jaipur

Jammu & Kashmir

Jasdan

Jhalawar

Jind pre-1885

Kishangarh

Las Bela

Morvi

Nandgaon

Nawanagar

Orchha

Poonch

Rajasthan
(overprint)

Rajpipla

Sirmoor

Soruth

Travancore

Travancore
Cochin

Wadhwan

D. Far East Scripts

Some difficult stamps for the new collector to identify are those from the countries of the Far East—China, Japan, Manchukuo, Ryukyu Islands and North and South Korea. China is further complicated because of the several different governments which have been in control (on the mainland and on the island of Taiwan, also known as Formosa). Parts of China have also been occupied by the Japanese and there are innumerable overprints and surcharges among China's prolific stamp issues. A preliminary study of the historical notes and the illustrations listed under China in the catalogue is recommended.

CHINA

A distinguishing emblem—the twelve-rayed sun—was used on Chinese stamps in pre-Communist times (up to 1949): note that it was also used on the stamps listed under the Japanese Occupation of China. In the Chinese language each character is a complete word: the various symbols are not letters of an alphabet. At one time the characters read downwards, one below the other, but nowadays sentences are more often written horizontally, though from right to left. In modern times—particularly under the Communist regime—the tendency is to write from left to right as in English. Look for the character *chung* (it is rather like a double-sided flag) at the beginning of the sentence (whether it is first or last) and count up to the third character—if it resembles a letter 'R' then the stamp is a pre-Communist issue. In the same location on stamps of the Communist People's Republic the character looks like an inverted 'V'. Most China (People's Republic) commemorative stamps have a serial number at the foot of the design, for example 'T. 108. (6–4) 1986'. This helps to aid rapid identification of Chinese issues.

The same rule applies to the stamps of Taiwan from 1949—the birth of the Chinese Nationalist Republic. Modern Taiwan stamps are inscribed 'Republic of China'.

China (1913)

China (People's Republic)

China (Taiwan)

JAPAN

Japanese is written in ideographic (picture-symbol) characters, acquired from China. Indeed, through constant contact with the Chinese people down the centuries (in peace and war), the Japanese language has enriched itself with Chinese words and expressions. Japanese stamps up to 1947 often had an emblem representing a chrysanthemum included in the design. And from 1966 the word 'Nippon' in our alphabet has been added to Japanese stamp designs. Inscriptions in the native language include the country name which comprises a standard group of four characters. The first of these (which may be last depending in which direction the sentence has been written) is easily recognizable—it resembles a box with a horizontal line through the middle (quite different to the Korean 'box').

In 1930 Japan alleged that her interests in Manchuria were being jeopardized by the Chinese and began the military occupation of the area, setting up a new puppet state of **Manchukuo**, consisting of the former provinces of Fegtien, Kirin, Heilungchiang and Jehol. President Pu Yi, who later became Emperor Kang-teh, was appointed

Head of State. The stamps, identified by the orchid crest and by the currency—100 fen = 1 yuan, are listed in the catalogue under China—Chinese Provinces—Manchuria.

Japan

RYUKYU ISLANDS

Ryukyu stamps, first issued in 1948, closely resembled those of Japan in style, inscriptions and currency—100 sen = 1 yen. The main inscription, however, lacks the box-like character noted above for Japan. Under United States administration the stamps were issued in American cents and dollars from 1958—note the distinctive '¢' for cents. From 1961 the word 'Ryukyus' appeared on the stamps which ceased in 1972 when the islands were handed back to Japan.

KOREA

The divided nation. Emblems and inscriptions help to distinguish the stamps of South and North Korea. Unlike Chinese, each sign in the Korean language is a separate letter of the alphabet—these are combined in groups to form complete characters. North Korean inscriptions have four such characters, those of South Korea have six, the first one resembling 'CH'. South Korean stamps additionally bear the *yin yang* symbol—a circle part light and part dark—and have been inscribed 'Republic of Korea' in English since 1966.

North Korea

Iran

E. Scripts Various

Nepal

Unfamiliar scripts and alphabets may present a problem if there is no other clue to a stamp's origins. Some are illustrated here as a general guide. Note the appearance and 'look' of an inscription, and observe particularly whether the script comprises separate characters (like the Amharic language from Ethiopia, or the Siamese language of Thailand which is derived from a form of Sanskrit and has affinities with Chinese), or in flowing style like Arabic or Persian, which is a version of Arabic. Most Arab countries inscribe their stamps additionally in English or French, but remember that Arabic is written from right to left and that there are six chief dialects—Algerian, Moroccan, Syrian, Egyptian, Iraqi and Arabian. The Turkish language, formerly written in Arabic characters, was changed to Roman by the order of Ataturk in 1928. Note also that Israel stamps, following the first 'Coins' issue of 1948, have been inscribed not only in Hebrew and Arabic, but in English as well.

Some of the Malay States are easy to identify with the names shown in English—Johore, Kedah, Malacca (or Melaka), Penang (or Pulau Pinang) and Sungei Ujong. But some have the state's name only in Malay script—which looks all 'dots and dashes' and has Arabic elements. These include Kelantan, Negri Sembilan (or Negeri Sembilan), Pahang, Perak, Perlis, Selangor and Trengganu. Look for a similar sultan's portrait or state arms in the catalogue. The Afghan languages are Persian or Pushtu (or Pashtu), but the stamps are usually inscribed in French—*Postes Afghanes*—as well as the native script. Nepali is the spoken language of the Gurkha peoples of Nepal, but all except the earliest stamps have been additionally inscribed 'Nepal' in English. Burmese, the language of the people of Burma, is allied to Chinese and is written in an alphabet derived from India, the characters of which are more or less circular and thereby easily identifiable on Burmese stamps in addition to the 'Burma Postage' or 'Union of Burma' inscriptions. The stamps of Sri Lanka (Ceylon) are unusual in that they are inscribed trilingually—Sinhalese, Tamil and English.

Afghanistan

Turkey

Brazil

Austria

Bosnia

Hungary

Portugal

Papal States

Sardinia

Spain

Switzerland

F. 'No-name' Stamps

As mentioned in the beginning, Great Britain is the only country in the world whose stamps do not bear the name of the issuing country, although all of them bear the likeness of the ruling monarch. In early days—before the foundation of the Universal Postal Union, other countries sometimes did not include their names. Three stamps which apparently defied the U.P.U. convention were issued by the United States in 1920, marking the tercentenary of the Landing of the Pilgrim Fathers—they omitted the customary 'U.S. Postage'.

Some 'difficult' countries are listed below with a number of the stamps illustrated.

Austria. Check the currencies on early issues because, although the designs are similar, your stamps might be from **Austrian Post Offices in Turkey**, or from **Lombardy and Venetia**. The head of Mercury, messenger of the gods, appears on Austrian newspaper stamps.

Bosnia and Herzegovina. The Austrian coat-of-arms is prominent.

Brazil. The early 'numeral' stamps represented 'Bull's-eyes', 'Goat's-eyes' and 'Snake's-eyes' respectively.

Finland. Circles in the designs distinguish the 1891 issue from the similar issues of Russia. Also issues between 1901 and 1911 bear the Finnish *penni* and *markkaa*.

Hungary. 1871–88. Similar to Austria, but the designs are distinctive.

Papal States. The crossed keys are the main clue. Cf. First issue of **Vatican City**.

Portugal. 'Correio', the 'reis' currency and the Royal heads suggest Portugal.

Sardinia. Compare with very similar stamps of **Italy**, 1862.

Spain. Stamps with various portraits, often inscribed *Comunicaciones*, sometimes dated, and with currencies in cuartos, centimos and pesetas, indicate 19th-century Spain, but should be checked with contemporary issues of **Cuba, Puerto Rico** or the **Philippines**, particularly if the inscription includes *Ultramar*.

Switzerland. Early postage dues were unnamed, being regarded as of internal significance only.